SCIENTIFIC AMERICAN EDUCATIONAL PUBLISHING

# SOUND SCIENCE

## 10 FUN SOUND EXPERIMENTS

I0811874

BRING SCIENCE HOME

Published in 2023 by The Rosen Publishing Group, Inc.
2455 Clinton Street, Buffalo, NY 14224

Copyright © 2023 by The Rosen Publishing Group, Inc.

First Edition

All rights reserved. No part of this book may be reproduced in any form without permission in writing from the publisher, except by a reviewer.

Editor: Jennifer Lombardo
Designer: Rachel Rising

Activity on page 5 by Science Buddies/Ben Finio; page 11 by Science Buddies/Sabine de Brabandere; page 17 by Science Buddies/Ben Finio; page 23 by Science Buddies/Megan Arnett; page 27 by Science Buddies/Sabine de Brabandere; page 33 by Science Buddies/Megan Arnett; page 39 by Science Buddies/Megan Arnett; page 45 by Science Buddies/Megan Arnett; page 51 by Science Buddies/Megan Arnett; page 56 by Science Buddies.

Photo Credits: pp. 3, 4, 5, 8, 9, 11, 14, 15, 17, 20, 23, 25, 27, 30, 31, 33, 37, 39, 43, 45, 48, 49, 51, 54, 56, 59, 60 cve iv/Shutterstock.com; pp. 5, 11, 17, 23, 27, 33, 39, 45, 51, 56 Anna Frajtova/Shutterstock.com.

All illustrations by Continuum Content Solutions

Cataloging-in-Publication Data
Names: Scientific American, inc.
Title: Sound science / edited by the Editors of Scientific American.
Description: Buffalo, New York : Scientific American Educational Publishing, 2023. | Series: Bring science home | Includes glossary and index.
Identifiers: ISBN 9781684169696 (pbk.) | ISBN 9781684169702 (library bound) | ISBN 9781684169719 (ebook)
Subjects: LCSH: Sound--Experiments--Juvenile literature. | Science projects--Juvenile literature.
Classification: LCC QC225.2 S686 2023 | DDC 534.078--dc23

Manufactured in the United States of America

Some of the images in this book illustrate individuals who are models. The depictions do not imply actual situations or events.

CPSIA Compliance Information: Batch #SACS23. For further information contact Rosen Publishing at 1-800-237-9932.

Find us on

# CONTENTS


Introduction .................................... 4

1. Make Your Own Speaker ........................ 5

2. What Do You Hear Underwater? ................. 11

3. Science with a Smartphone: Decibel Meter ..... 17

4. Tune Up Your Rubber Band Guitar! ............. 23

5. Crash, Clunk, Thump—Let's Make Some Noise! ... 27

6. Sound Science: Make Your Own Harmonica! ...... 33

7. Ring on the Resonance! ....................... 39

8. Hanging Around with Sound:
Make Your Own Secret Bell! ...................... 45

9. Can You Kazoo? ............................... 51

10. Making Sound Waves .......................... 56

The Scientific Method ........................... 61

Glossary ........................................ 62

Additional Resources ............................ 63

Index ........................................... 64


These activities include science fair project ideas.

# INTRODUCTION

What are sound waves? How do they travel? How do musical instruments work? Science can answer all of these questions and many more. Use the experiments in this book to observe how sound works and to learn what you can do to change the sounds you're hearing. You'll never think of sound the same way again!

Projects marked with ⚛ include a section called Science Fair Ideas. These ideas can help you develop your own original science fair project. Science fair judges tend to reward creative thought and imagination, and it helps if you are really interested in your project.

You will also need to follow the scientific method when developing and carrying out a science fair project. See page 61 for more information about that.

# Make Your Own Speaker

TURN IT UP—WITH A LITTLE PHYSICS!

Do you like to listen to music? Have you ever wondered how a TV, computer, or phone turns music into sound that your ears can hear? In this project, you will build your own speaker from household materials and find out how speakers convert electrical signals into sound.

## PROJECT TIME

60 to 80 minutes

## KEY CONCEPTS

Physics
Sound
Magnetism
Electricity

## BACKGROUND

Sounds, such as songs or the audio track on a movie, can be stored as an electronic file. The data in the file shows how the loudness and pitch of the sound changes over time. This information can be sent electronically through a wire (or in the case of a Wi-Fi signal, through the air using radio waves). This process moves the information from one place to another in digital form—but it does not produce a sound.

To make sound from an electrical signal, we need another piece of the puzzle: electromagnetism. When an electrical current flows through a wire, it produces a magnetic field around the wire. The magnetic field around a single, straight piece of wire is fairly weak. Wrapping a bunch of wire into a tight coil, however, can make the magnetic field much stronger. So when we send the changing electrical signal from an audio file through a wire coil, we get a changing magnetic field that corresponds to the original sound.

This changing magnetic field can push and pull on the magnetic field of a nearby magnet (called the permanent magnet). When magnets push and pull on each other, they can create motion. You've noticed this if you have ever snapped two magnets together or used one magnet to push another magnet away. When one of the magnets (either the electromagnet or the permanent magnet) is attached to a thin membrane, the rapidly changing magnetic field makes the membrane vibrate. The vibrating membrane bumps into nearby air molecules, causing them to vibrate as well. This vibration travels through the air as a sound wave. Eventually, it reaches your ears, and you hear a sound.

Normally, speakers are covered in a case or built into an electronic device, so you can't see inside them. In this project, you will build your own speakers from scratch so you can see how they work!

## MATERIALS

- Electronic device (phone, tablet, computer, and so on) with a headphone jack and the ability to play music
- 3.5-millimeter stereo cable (a typical "headphone" plug) that can be cut and modified
- Neodymium magnet (also called a "rare earth" magnet) that is approximately 0.5 inch (1.3 cm) in diameter and 0.5 inch (1.3 cm) long; this can be purchased at a hardware store or online. (These can be dangerous if accidentally swallowed, so keep them away from little kids.)

- At least 6 feet (2 m) of 30-gauge magnet wire (also called enameled wire), which also can be purchased at a hardware store or online. Make sure the wire is insulated and not bare copper.
- At least one paper or plastic cup
- Clear tape
- Scissors
- Fine grit sandpaper
- Adult helper
- Wire strippers (optional)

## PREPARATION

- Carefully cut your 3.5-mm audio (headphone) cable in half. Ask an adult to help you strip off about 2 inches (5 cm) of the outer insulation from the cut end. You can do this using wire strippers or by scraping the insulation off with scissors.
- There should be three smaller wires inside the cable. Usually, there will be one bare copper wire (this is the "ground" wire) and two other insulated wires: one red and one white (which are the left and right audio signals for a stereo system).
- Strip the insulation off about 2 inches (5 cm) of one of the audio wires (it does not matter which).

## PROCEDURE

- Make a coil of wire by wrapping the magnet wire around your finger about 50 times (making sure not to wrap it so tightly that you cut off the circulation!). Leave at least 6 inches (15 cm) of wire loose at both ends of the coil.
- Tape the coil flat to the outside bottom of your cup. Make sure the coil does not unravel.
- Use fine grit sandpaper to strip the insulation off about 2 inches (5 cm) of each end of the wire.

- Tightly twist each end of your coil wire to one of the stripped wires from the 3.5-mm audio cable. The wires need to be in good electrical contact with each other, so they cannot be loose.
- Wrap each twisted wire connection in tape. Completely cover all the exposed wire where you stripped off insulation. This will help prevent short circuits.
- Plug the other end of the 3.5-mm cable into your electronic device's headphone jack. Start playing a song.
- Hold the cup up to your ear with one hand.
- Hold the neodymium magnet directly below the coil at the outside bottom of the cup so it is almost touching. *Can you hear the song playing?*
- Try slowly moving the magnet closer to or farther away from the coil. *How does the loudness of the music change?*
- Troubleshooting: If you do not hear anything, double check to make sure your wires are tightly twisted together and not loose. Make sure the volume on your electronic device is turned up all the way.

## SCIENCE FAIR IDEA

Try using a bigger magnet (or multiple magnets stacked end to end) or wrapping a new coil with more turns of wire. *Can you make your speaker louder?*

## SCIENCE FAIR IDEA

Strip both audio wires in the 3.5-mm cable. Build and connect a second speaker (connect one end of the coil wire to the ground cable and the other end to the new audio wire—so both of your speakers will be connected to the ground wire). *Can you build "headphones" so you can wear both speakers on your ears?*

## OBSERVATIONS AND RESULTS

When you held your speaker up to your ear and held the magnet near the coil, you should have been able to hear very faint music. If you moved the magnet away, the music would disappear. This happens because magnetic forces are very strong close to the magnet but quickly get weaker farther away from the magnet.

Unlike a regular speaker, your speaker was probably not loud enough for you to hear it from across the room. Regular speakers usually have a separate power supply (they plug into a wall outlet or a USB port, or they have an internal battery) and an amplifier, which makes the sound much louder. Your speaker functions more like wired headphones, which don't have an external power supply. You can hear sound from headphones when you put the earbuds directly into your ear, but not from across the room.

## CLEANUP

Put away any leftover materials, and throw out any scraps, such as the insulation you scraped off the wires.

# What Do You Hear Underwater?

MAKE WAVES—UNDERWATER! LEARN HOW SOUND TRAVELS DIFFERENTLY IN WATER THAN IT DOES IN THE AIR.

Have you ever listened to noises underwater? Sound travels differently in the water than it does in the air. To learn more, try making your own underwater noises—and listening carefully.

## PROJECT TIME

30 to 45 minutes

## KEY CONCEPTS

Physics
Sound waves
Biology

## BACKGROUND

Sound is a wave created by vibrations. These vibrations create areas of more and less densely packed particles. So sound needs a medium to travel, such as air, water, or even solids.

Sound waves travel faster in denser substances because neighboring particles will more easily bump into one another. Take water, for example. There are about 800 times more particles in a bottle of water than there are in the same bottle filled with air. Thus sound waves travel much faster in water than they do in air. In freshwater at room temperature, for example, sound travels about 4.3 times faster than it does in air at the same temperature.

Sound traveling through air soon becomes less loud as you get farther from the source. This is because the waves' energy quickly gets lost along the way. Sound keeps its energy longer when traveling through water because the particles can carry the sound waves better. In the ocean, for example, the sound of a humpback whale can travel thousands of miles!

Underwater sound waves reaching us at a faster pace and keeping their intensity longer seem like they should make us perceive those sounds as louder when we are also underwater. The human ear, however, evolved to hear sound in the air and is not as useful when submerged in water. Our head itself is full of tissues that contain water and can transmit sound waves when we are underwater. When this happens, the vibrations bypass the eardrum, the part of the ear that evolved to pick up sound waves in the air.

Sound also interacts with boundaries between two different mediums, such as the surface of water. This boundary between water and air, for example, reflects almost all sounds back into the water. How will all these dynamics influence how we perceive underwater sounds? Try the activity to find out!

## MATERIALS

- Bathtub or swimming pool (a very large bucket can work too)
- Water
- Two stainless steel utensils (for example, spoons or tongs)
- Two plastic utensils
- Small ball
- Towel
- Adult helper
- An area that can get wet (if not performing the activity at a pool)

- Floor cloth to clean up spills (if not performing the activity at a pool)
- Other materials to make underwater sounds (optional)
- Access to a swimming pool (optional)
- Internet access (optional)

## PREPARATION

- Fill the bathtub with lukewarm water—or head to the pool—and bring your helper and other materials.

## PROCEDURE

- Ask your helper to click one stainless steel utensil against another. Listen. *How would you describe the sound?*
- In a moment, your helper will click one utensil against the other underwater. *Do you think you will hear the same sound?*
- Ask your helper to click one utensil against the other underwater. Listen. *Does the sound appear to be louder or softer? Is what you hear different in other ways too?*
- Safely submerge one ear in the water. Ask your helper to click one utensil against the other underwater. Listen. *How would you describe this sound?*
- Ask your helper to click one utensil against the other underwater soon after you submerge your head. Take a deep breath, close your eyes, and safely submerge your head completely or as much as you feel comfortable doing. Listen while you hold your breath underwater (come up for air when you need to!). *Does the sound appear to be louder or softer? Does it appear to be different in other ways?*

- Repeat this sequence, but have your helper use two plastic utensils banging against each other instead.
- Repeat the sequence again, but this time listen to a small ball being dropped into the water. *Does the sound of a ball falling into the water change when you listen above or below the water? Does your perception of this sound change? Why would this happen?*
- Switch roles. Have your helper listen while you make the sounds.
- Discuss the findings you gathered. *Do patterns appear? Can you conclude something about how humans perceive sounds when submerged in water?*

## SCIENCE FAIR IDEA

Test with more types of sounds: soft as well as loud sounds, high- and low-pitched sounds. *Can you find more patterns?*

## SCIENCE FAIR IDEA

To investigate what picks up the sound wave when you are submerged, use your fingers to close your ears or use earplugs when submerging your head. *How does the sound change when you close off your ear canal underwater? Does the same happen when you close off your ear canal when you are above water? If not, why would this be different?*

## SCIENCE FAIR IDEA

If you can, go to a swimming pool, and listen to the sound of someone jumping into the water. Compare your perception of the sound when you are submerged with when your head is above the water. *How does your perception change? Close your eyes. Can you tell where the person jumped into the water when submerged? Can you tell when you have your head above the water?*

## SCIENCE FAIR IDEA

Research ocean sounds and how sounds caused by human activity impact aquatic animals.

## OBSERVATIONS AND RESULTS

Was the sound softer when it was created underwater and you listened above the water? Did it sound muffled when you had only your ear submerged? Was it fuller when you had your head submerged?

Sound travels faster in water compared with air because water particles are packed in more densely. Thus, the energy the sound waves carry is transported faster. This should make the sound appear louder. You probably perceived it as softer when you were not submerged, however, because the water surface is almost like a mirror for the sound you created. The sound most likely almost completely reflected back into the water as soon as it reached the surface.

When you submerged only your ear, the sound probably still appeared muffled. This happens because the human ear is not good at picking up sound in water—after all, it evolved to pick up sound in air.

When you submerged your head, the sound probably sounded fuller. That is because our head contains a lot of water, which allows the tissues in our head to pick up underwater sound—without relying on the eardrum. It also explains why closing your ear canal makes almost no difference in the sound you pick up while you are underwater.

If you tried to detect where the sound came from when submerged, you probably had a hard time. Our brain uses the difference in loudness and timing of the sound detected by each ear as a clue to infer where the sound came from. Because sound travels faster underwater and because you pick up sound with your entire head when you are submerged, your brain loses the cues that normally help you determine where the sound is coming from.

## CLEANUP

Wipe up any water you may have spilled, and put away the objects you used to make noise.

# Science with a Smartphone: Decibel Meter

LOUD AND CLEAR: SEE HOW YOUR VOICE AND THE VOICES OF OTHERS MEASURE UP BY TESTING NOISE LEVELS WITH A DECIBEL METER.

Did you know that you can use a smartphone as a scientific instrument to explore the world around you? Smartphones contain many built-in electronic sensors that can measure phenomena such as sound, light, motion, and more! In this activity you'll use a phone's microphone to examine the loudness of different sounds in your environment. How quiet is a library? How loud is that truck roaring by? Try this activity to find out!

## PROJECT TIME

30 to 45 minutes

## KEY CONCEPTS

Physics
Sound
Measurement
Logarithms

## BACKGROUND

You're probably familiar with the units we use to measure everyday quantities, such as length or temperature. You wouldn't bat an eye at someone saying they are 6 feet (1.8 m) tall or it's 70 degrees outside. However, how do we measure sound? You might describe a sound as "quiet as a whisper" or "louder than a jet engine," but you probably wouldn't use a number. Sound is measured using a unit called decibels, abbreviated dB. The decibel scale is a little unusual because it is logarithmic rather than linear. What does that mean? For every increase of 10 dB, the loudness of the sound doubles. For example, a 30 dB sound is twice as loud as a 20 dB sound. A 40 dB sound is twice as loud as a 30 dB sound, and four times as loud as a 20 dB sound. Zero dB doesn't mean there is no sound at all. Rather, 0 dB is chosen as a reference level at the threshold of human hearing. Sound confusing? Don't worry—here's a list of reference sounds and their approximate decibel levels:

0 dB: human hearing threshold
20 dB: rustling leaves
40 dB: quiet library
60 dB: normal conversation
80 dB: screaming baby
100 dB: chain saw
120 dB: live rock concert
140 dB: jet engine

Sound levels above 80 dB can cause hearing damage over long periods of time, and sound levels above 120 dB can cause immediate damage. That's why hearing protection is recommended for people using equipment such as lawn mowers. Note the loudness of a sound also depends on your distance from the source of the sound (it will get quieter as you get farther away)—so to do a direct comparison of different sounds, you have to keep this distance constant.

What does all this have to do with a smartphone? If you wanted to measure sound levels previously, you would have had to buy a decibel meter—a device with a microphone and a screen that would display the sound level in dB. Modern smartphones (which already contain built-in microphones) can run apps that will display the sound reading in dB directly on the phone's screen. So if you want to explore the sounds of the world around you, all you need is a phone!

## MATERIALS

- Smartphone or tablet with internet access and permission to download and install an app

- Adult (to help verify and download the app)
- Other people whose voices you can measure (optional)
- Multiple locations to take the phone (optional)

## PREPARATION

- Ask an adult to help you search for a "decibel meter" or "sound meter" app on a smartphone or tablet. There are plenty of free options available, but some apps may have ads or in-app purchases enabled.
- Get to know your decibel meter app. Some apps will just display a number on the screen, whereas others will display a meter or a graph. Some will also let you record data. Make sure the app is working: Talk at a normal volume, and you should see the numbers fluctuate.

## PROCEDURE

- Determine the level of background noise. Put the phone down, sit perfectly still and hold your breath. *What is the decibel level? Does it fluctuate with background noises, such as a car driving by or a bird chirping?*
- Now explore your own voice. Try whispering, talking and even yelling at the phone. You can also try other sounds, such as whistling or humming. *Does the whisper even register, or is it drowned out by the background noise? How loud is your yell?*
- If there are other people around, try measuring their voices as well. *Is everyone's "normal" voice the same decibel level? Who can yell the loudest?*

- Now test different sounds. This can be as simple as clapping your hands or knocking on a door. There are plenty of other everyday sounds you can try as well—for instance, running a faucet or clicking a light switch. You can also try running some appliances, such as a microwave or vacuum. *How do all the different sounds compare? Which ones are the loudest?*
- Find out how distance from the sound source affects the sound level. Try to find a relatively constant sound, such as a running faucet or a person humming. Start out with the phone right next to the source, and then slowly walk away. *How does the decibel level change as you get farther away?*
- Try measuring background noise levels in different locations. Take the phone into different rooms, to a library, or to a playground or park. *Where is the quietest place you can find? The loudest? Are noise levels loud enough anywhere that they could pose a danger to your hearing?*

## SCIENCE FAIR IDEA

You can also download apps to measure the frequency, or pitch, of sounds. Frequency is measured in hertz (Hz). The range of human hearing is from about 20 to 20,000 Hz. As we get older, we tend to lose our ability to hear sounds at the higher end of that range. Some animals, such as dogs, can hear all the way up to 45,000 Hz. *What's the frequency range of your voice? What about all the other sounds you measured earlier?*

## SCIENCE FAIR IDEA

Measure the sounds made by various musical instruments. If you don't have any instruments handy, you can make your own!

## OBSERVATIONS AND RESULTS

Using everyday items, you could probably measure sounds in the range of roughly 20 to 80 dB. Even in a perfectly "quiet" room, background noises, such as the hum of a computer or even your own breathing, could make it hard to get below about 10 dB. If you're in a busier location with lots of people or you are close to a street with lots of traffic, the background noise level would probably be much higher. Loud appliances, such as a vacuum cleaner or power tools, could exceed 80 dB. Human screams can be quite loud, possibly exceeding 100 dB (as of March 2019, the world record is 129 dB!)—but you probably want to avoid that because screams that loud can hurt your ears! You should also have found sound levels drop off quickly as you get farther from the source. People who will be very close to a consistently loud sound all day (such as someone who mows lawns or works near jet engines for a living) should wear hearing protection.

### CLEANUP

Turn off any appliances you may have turned on.

# Tune Up Your Rubber Band Guitar!

MAKE SOME NOISE! LEARN HOW PHYSICS IS BEHIND EVERY GUITAR NOTE—BY MAKING YOUR OWN INSTRUMENT.

Did you know the modern guitar is an instrument that dates back more than 4,000 years? The first written guitar music was published in the 16th century, during a time when guitars still had strings made from animal intestines! Although guitars have a long history, they are still extremely popular in modern music. Have you ever wondered how they make the music you listen to? In this activity, we'll make our own guitars and test the different sounds we can create.

## PROJECT TIME

45 to 60 minutes

## KEY CONCEPTS

Physics
Sound
Frequency
Pitch

## BACKGROUND

Sounds travel to our ears as sound waves—vibrations in the air we perceive as sound. These waves are generated by the vibration or movement of an object in a medium. They most commonly reach us by traveling via the air, although they can also pass through liquids and solids—that's why you can hear things underwater or if you press your ear up against a wall. A vibrating object, such as a tuning fork, generates a sound wave. The fork's vibrations cause the air particles around it to vibrate at the same frequency. These air particles bump into the air particles around them, and the sound wave propagates outward from the tuning fork.

When a guitarist plucks a guitar string, it vibrates at a specific frequency, which determines the pitch of the sound we hear. Faster vibrations produce higher-pitched sounds. Children generally have smaller, thinner vocal cords that vibrate much faster than those of adults. As a result, children's voices sound much higher.

In this activity, you will build your own guitar and explore how frequency changes the pitch of the sound we hear. Time to tune up!

## MATERIALS

- Four rubber bands of varying thickness but the same length
- Glue
- Packing tape (or other strong tape)
- Empty rectangular tissue box
- Scissors
- Two large craft sticks
- Empty paper towel tube

## PREPARATION

- Remove the plastic inside the hole of the tissue box.
- Use the tape to attach the paper towel tube to one short end of the tissue box. Make sure it is lined up with the box's hole.
- Glue a craft stick to each end of the hole in the tissue box. The sticks should be perpendicular to the direction of the hole and close to its edges. Allow the glue to dry.

## PROCEDURE

- Wrap each rubber band around the tissue box lengthwise so they rest on the craft sticks. The rubber bands can cross over the hole in the tissue box top, but they don't need to as long as they're resting on the craft sticks.
- Hold your guitar by the paper towel roll, and gently pluck each rubber band. *Do all of the rubber bands sound the same? If not, which makes a higher-pitched sound, the thin or thick rubber bands? In addition to sound, can you feel anything happening when you pluck the rubber bands?*
- Choose one rubber band, and pluck it. Listen carefully to the sound it makes. Press your finger down on the rubber band so that it is pinched between your finger and one of the craft sticks. *Does the sound change when your finger is pressed on the rubber band? If so, what changes about it?*
- Try pressing each rubber band down on the craft stick. Notice how this changes the sound the rubber band makes.

### SCIENCE FAIR IDEA

Try increasing the size of the tissue box hole. *How does this change the sound?*

## OBSERVATIONS AND RESULTS

The sound made by your instrument was the sound created by the rubber band vibrating when you plucked it, much like how a real guitar string vibrates when played by a musician. As you strummed the strings of your instrument, you might have noticed you could feel the vibrations of the rubber band traveling through the tissue box.

The thickness of the rubber band changed the tone of the sound you heard when you plucked it. The thinner strings on a guitar make a higher-pitched sound because they can vibrate more quickly than the thicker ones. The thinner strings on your rubber band guitar are the same—they vibrate more quickly, and we perceive these vibrations as a higher-pitched sound.

When you held the rubber band down, the sound changed, and eventually there was no sound at all. From this, you could observe the sound was created by the rubber band—and when you prevented the rubber band from moving, you couldn't produce any sound.

In addition, in this activity, you should have noticed you could change the pitch of the sound by pressing down on the rubber band. When you pressed down on it, the vibrating section of the rubber band got shorter. As a result, the pitch of the sound got higher.

## CLEANUP

Put your newly made guitar away, and clean up any mess you may have made while you were making it.

# Crash, Clunk, Thump
## Let's Make Some Noise!

LEARN ABOUT THE SCIENCE OF SOUND VIBRATION WITH THIS FREE-FALL PHYSICS ACTIVITY!

Have you ever thought about the sheer number of words that exist in the English language to describe sounds? A noise can be a thud, a clang, a bang, a pop, a crash, a splash, a clatter, a buzz, a tinkle, and many more! You can probably think of an example for each of these—but if you heard the sound, could you say what produced it?

### PROJECT TIME

20 to 40 minutes

### KEY CONCEPTS

Physics
Sound
Vibrations
Material science

## BACKGROUND

Start to hum and then touch the front of your throat. Can you feel it vibrate? That vibration from your throat also occurs in the air, which your ears pick up and, together with your brain, translate it into the humming sound you hear. This sequence occurs with any sound you hear: It starts with a vibration, which is carried by one or more media (air, water, the wall, etc.) to your ears. Your ears register the vibration and transmit it as nerve impulses to your brain, which converts it into the sound you hear.

We hear a wealth of sounds. This is because vibrations come in a wide variety, and they all influence tone, which consists of sound quality, pitch, and volume. Fast or slow vibrations are perceived as high- or low-pitched sounds, respectively. Each musical note has a specific pitch, but tones with the same pitch can sound very different. For example, the middle C on a piano does not sound the same as the middle C on a guitar, a violin, or a flute because these objects each vibrate in a complex way. There are many faster vibrations—called overtones—on top of the main vibration, each with their own volume.

When a hard material crashes onto a hard floor, the sudden impact makes it vibrate and creates a sound with a particular tone. If the same object is dropped again, the crash sounds similar because the object vibrates in a similar way. This might make you wonder if you can tell what object dropped, what it is made of, how heavy it is, or its shape just by listening to the sound it makes when you drop it. Try this activity to find out if you can!

## MATERIALS

- At least two objects, each made from a different material, that you can drop without worrying about breaking them or damaging the surface or floor. Choose from the following materials: hard plastic (for example, a spoon, a cup); metal (silverware, serving plates); and wood (serving spoon, blocks)
- Bag to hold your items
- Hard floor (tile or wood) or another hard surface such as a countertop or table (Make sure you have permission to drop things on these surfaces—some objects could cause scratches.)
- Carpeted floor (A thick carpet works best.)
- Partner

## PREPARATION

- Show the objects you will use in your experiment to your partner. Gather these objects in a bag and walk to the area with the hard floor or surface.
- Ask your partner to face away from you so he or she cannot see what you do.
- Explain to your partner that you will pick an object out of your bag and drop it on the floor. He or she needs to listen to the crash and, from the sound, identify what the dropped object is. *Do you think your partner will know what you dropped? Why do you think this?*

## PROCEDURE

- Pick a metal object from the bag, and drop it so it makes a sound when crashing onto the floor. Repeat this a few times so your partner can hear the sound well. Ask your partner what you just dropped. *Can he or she tell? If not, did your partner pick one made of the same material or one that is similar in shape or weight?*
- Show your partner what you dropped.
- Put the object back in the bag, pick a plastic object from the bag, and repeat the sequence.
- Put the plastic object back in the bag, pick a wooden object from it, then repeat the sequence.
- Put the wooden object back in the bag, randomly pick another object from it, and repeat the sequence. Do this a few times. *Do you see a pattern in what your partner can identify? Is it easy to know what you dropped? Does he or she frequently pick an object made of the same material, the same shape, or the same weight? Why do you think this is the case?*

- Switch roles. Now, your partner will drop objects, and you will guess what they are. *Do you think it will be easier for you to identify the objects because you just heard the sounds these objects make when crashing onto the ground?*
- Perform the tests.
- *Do you see a pattern in what you can identify? Is it easy to tell what was dropped? Do you frequently pick an object made of the same material, the same shape, or the same weight? Why do you think you can or cannot do this?*
- *Is your pattern similar to your partner's?*
- *Do you think the results of these tests would have been different if you had dropped objects on a carpeted floor instead? Why do you think this is the case?*
- Move to an area covered with carpet, and try the same tests. *Can you or your partner distinguish what fell just by hearing the crash? If not, can you distinguish the material, the shape, or the weight of the falling object? Why is this so?*

## SCIENCE FAIR IDEA

*What noise does a soft object, such as a scarf, make when landing on the ground? Why is this so?*

## SCIENCE FAIR IDEA

Investigate if you can distinguish between heavy and light objects made of the same material crashing onto a hard floor or between hollow and filled objects made of the same material.

## SCIENCE FAIR IDEA

*Can you find words to describe the different sounds you produced in this activity?*

## OBSERVATIONS AND RESULTS

You and your partner could probably identify what the falling object was made of (wood, metal, or plastic), but it was probably harder to guess what the object was exactly.

When hard objects crash onto a hard surface, the vibrations from the sudden impact are like a person on a swing: After an initial push, they will swing back and forth, a little lower each time, until they eventually stop. Similarly, the dropped object gets a push at impact and starts vibrating, but the movements are too small for you to see. They become smaller and smaller until they eventually stop. These vibrations create rhythmic disturbances in the air. Your ears pick up these disturbances, and that is how you hear the sound of the crash.

Because materials vibrate in many ways and our ears are designed to register tiny differences, we hear a variety of sounds. A metal object crashing onto a hard floor will vibrate in a specific way, creating a specific sound. Other metal objects will vibrate in a similar—but not identical—way, creating a similar sound. You learned to distinguish the sounds of metal, plastic, and wooden objects crashing onto a hard floor, which is why you could probably tell what the falling objects were made of.

Heavier objects vibrate differently compared with lighter ones. (This also is true for hollow versus full or short versus long ones.) The sounds these types of crashes make are different, but they are often harder to tell apart. You might have had trouble differentiating the sounds made by two different objects of the same material if they were close in size or shape. When we drop soft materials onto a hard floor or drop a hard material onto a soft, carpeted floor, the resulting vibrations are not as big. That is why these crashes are not as noisy.

## CLEANUP

**Put away the objects you used.**

# Sound Science
## Make Your Own Harmonica!

RING IN THE NEW YEAR WITH THIS FUN, PHYSICS-POWERED HOMEMADE INSTRUMENT!

Can you name the bestselling musical instrument in the world? If you said harmonica, you're right! The harmonica was patented in 1821 by a 16-year-old German boy. Since then, it's become the top selling instrument in the world and a household item in many places. It's easy to take instruments (and the music they make) for granted, but creating beautiful noise is not just an art—it's also a science! In this activity, you will design and explore your own harmonica-like instrument made from household items. Time to tune up!

### PROJECT TIME

60 to 75 minutes

### KEY CONCEPTS

Physics
Sound waves
Frequency
Pitch
Hertz

## BACKGROUND

The sounds we hear every day are sound waves traveling through the air and reaching our ears. Sound waves are generated by the vibration or movement of an object in a medium. Sound waves most commonly reach us by traveling through the air. The sound wave originates from the vibrating object, such as a vocal chord, and travels through the medium (such as air), causing all of the air particles to vibrate at the frequency of the vocal chord. The frequency of this movement is commonly measured in Hertz (Hz), where 1 Hertz equals 1 vibration per second.

To help understand this, imagine two people holding a rope between them. If one person gently shakes the rope up and down 1 time per second, a wave will travel through the rope with a frequency of 1 Hz. If the person increases their speed so they are moving the rope up and down 2 times per second, a wave will travel through the rope at a frequency of 2 Hz.

Sound travels through the air in a similar manner. A violinist runs a bow over the strings of the violin, causing the strings to vibrate. The vibrating string bumps against the air particles all around it. These air particles subsequently bump against air particles next to them and so forth, so the wave travels from air particle to air particle—all at the same frequency as the vibration of the violin string.

In this activity, you will create your own sonorous instrument and explore the kinds of sound waves it generates.

## MATERIALS

- Two large craft sticks (at least 6 inches [15 cm], long)
- Two wide rubber bands (#64 size works well)
- One plastic drinking straw
- Four small rubber bands
- A ruler
- Scissors
- An adult helper
- A piece of paper
- A pen or pencil

## PREPARATION

- Stretch the wide rubber band over one of the craft sticks lengthwise.
- Use your scissors to cut four pieces of straw, each 1 to 1.5 inches (2.5 to 4 cm) long.
- Place one of the straw pieces under the rubber band perpendicular to the craft stick. Move this straw so that it is about 2 inches (5 cm) from the end of the craft stick. This is Straw 1.
- Moving away from the end of the craft stick, place another straw piece on top of the rubber band next to Straw 1. This is Straw 2.
- Place the third straw piece next to Straw 2, under the rubber band. This is Straw 3.
- Place the last straw piece next to Straw 3, on top of the rubber band. This is Straw 4.
- Straw 1 and Straw 4 should be closest to the ends of the craft stick, whereas Straws 2 and 3 should be in the middle.
- With an adult to help you hold the straws in place, put the second craft stick on top of the of the first one, creating a sandwich with the straws in between the craft sticks.
- Secure this sandwich by wrapping a small rubber band approximately 0.5 inch (1 cm) from each end of the sticks. The ends of the sticks should be pinched together with a small space between them created by the straws.
- Use your paper and pencil to draw a table with two columns and five rows. Label the first column "distance between middle straws" and fill in each space below with: "2.5 inches (6 cm)," "2 inches (5 cm)," "1.5 inches (4 cm)" and "1 inch (2.5 cm)." Label the second column "tone of sound."

## PROCEDURE

- To start, move Straws 1 and 4 as close to the ends of the craft stick as possible. You can move the straws by gently sliding them back and forth, being careful not to pull them out of the sandwich!
- Slide Straws 2 and 3 away from each other so that there is a distance of 2.5 inches (6 cm) between them.
- Hold your instrument as though it is a sandwich, with one hand gently holding each end and the open part facing toward you. Make sure that the craft stick with the rubber band is on the bottom of your sandwich, and try to keep your fingers on the small rubber band. Make sure you aren't pressing down on the wide rubber band.
- Blow through the opening between the craft sticks as though it is a harmonica (don't blow through the straws!). *What sound do you hear? Do you feel anything as you blow through your instrument? Do the craft sticks vibrate or feel different when you play a sound?*
- Move Straws 2 and 3 closer together, so that there is a distance of 2 inches (5 cm) between them.
- Again, blow through your instrument. Notice the sound and the feeling in your hands. *Does this sound different than the first time you played it? If so, in what way? Does the vibration of the instrument feel any different?*
- Again, move Straws 2 and 3 closer together so that there is a distance of 1.5 inches (4 cm) between them.
- Blow through your instrument. Notice the sound and the feeling in your hands. *Does this sound different than the other times you played it? If so, in what way? Does the vibration of the instrument feel any different?*
- Finally, move Straws 2 and 3 closer together again so that there is a distance of 1 inch (2.5 cm) between them.

- Once again, blow through your instrument. Notice the sound and the feeling in your hands. *Does this sound different than the other times you played it? If so, in what way? Does the vibration of the instrument feel any different?*

- Return Straws 2 and 3 to their original position, with 2.5 inches (6 cm) between them. Repeat the above steps—this time recording your observations about the tone of the sound in your table. To help you compare the sounds, rate the lowest-pitched sound as a 1 and the highest-pitched sound as a 4.

- Consider the results in your table. *Do you notice any patterns in the tone of the sound? Did the tone change as you moved the straws? If so, did moving the straws closer to each other make the tone higher or lower?*

- Flip your instrument over so that the wide rubber band is on top. Hold the instrument so that your fingers are pressing down on the wide rubber band. Blow through your instrument as you have for previous steps. *Does holding the rubber band change anything about your instrument? How would you explain any differences you observe?*

- Flip the instrument back over so that the rubber band is on the bottom again. Remove all of the straws except for Straw 1. Try blowing through your instrument. *Does this sound different than the other times you played it? If so, in what way? Does the vibration of the instrument feel any different?*

- Try moving the remaining straw and observing how this affects the tone of the sound. *Can you change the tone of the sound by moving the straw?*

## SCIENCE FAIR IDEA

Test larger and/or smaller craft sticks and materials other than the straws. *How many different instruments can you make?*

## OBSERVATIONS AND RESULTS

The sound made by your instrument is actually the sound created by the large rubber band vibrating as you blow through it, much as a violin string vibrates when played by a violinist. As you blew through your instrument, you might have noticed that you could feel the vibrating rubber band through the craft stick. In addition, when you flipped the instrument over and pressed down on the rubber band, you probably found that you could not produce any sound when you blew through it. From this, you can observe that the sound is created by the rubber band, and when you prevent the rubber band from moving, you can't produce any sound.

In addition, in this activity you should have noticed that you could change the tone of the sound by moving the straws. When you moved Straws 2 and 3 closer together, the vibrating section of the rubber band got shorter. As a result, the tone of the sound got higher. The shorter rubber band vibrates more quickly, and our ears pick up these faster frequencies as a higher-pitched sound. The thinner strings on a violin make a higher-pitched sound because they can vibrate more quickly than the thicker strings. Similarly, men tend to have longer vocal chords than women, and therefore their voices are generally lower than women's voices.

When you removed all but one straw, you should have found that the sound of the instrument became lower. With only one straw, the rubber band was longer, and the sound it made when it vibrated was lower. As you moved the remaining straw, you could change the tone as the rubber band became shorter and longer.

## CLEANUP

Put your materials away, and throw out any scraps.

# Ring on the Resonance!

MAKE SOME REAL MOVES WITH RESONANCE! FIND OUT HOW PHYSICS EXPLAINS WHY SOME OBJECTS PREFER TO "MOVE" AT CERTAIN RATES.

Have you ever been on a swing set and suddenly noticed that the person on the swing next to you seems to be swinging almost exactly in time with you? You go up and down at either the same time or exactly opposite each other. This might seem random—but it's actually physics! Like many things in nature, swing sets have a resonant frequency, which means they have a "favorite" frequency (or speed) of movement. The swing set will naturally want to swing at its favorite speed. You might have experienced this if someone has ever tried to push you too fast on the swing; The preferred speed can actually make you go slower.
In this activity, we'll use paper rings (and lots of shaking) to examine resonant frequencies for ourselves!

## PROJECT TIME

60 to 75 minutes

## KEY CONCEPTS

Physics
Resonance
Resonant frequency
Vibration

## BACKGROUND

If you've ever played a guitar, violin, or other string instrument, you've seen resonant frequency in action. A single guitar string, when plucked, will vibrate at its resonant, or favorite, frequency. The vibration of the string creates a sound wave, which we hear as a note. It's always the same note for the same string because that string (when tuned correctly) always vibrates at its resonant frequency.

Resonant frequency is determined by several factors, including the mass of the object and the stiffness of the object. Again, if you've ever played a guitar, you may have noticed that the strings aren't all the same. The low E string is much thicker than the high E string. Because it is thicker, the low E string's resonant frequency is lower (or slower) than the thinner high E string. In this activity, we'll observe how mass and stiffness affect the resonant frequency of different size rings. Get ready to shake things up!

## MATERIALS

- Scissors
- 4 sheets of construction paper (ideally four different colors)
- Tape
- Piece of cardboard (about 5 by 12 inches [13 by 30.5 cm])
- Ruler

## PREPARATION

- Cut seven lengthwise strips (about 1 inch [2.5 cm] wide) from the construction paper; cut two strips from the first three colors and one strip from the fourth.
- Use tape to connect the same colored strips, forming three long strips, each about 22 inches (56 cm) long.

- Keep one strip 22 inches (56 cm) long. Trim about 3 inches (7.5 cm) from the second strip and 6 inches (15 cm) from the third one. Combined with the strip cut from the fourth sheet, you should have four strips of paper with lengths of 22, 19, 16 and 12 inches (56, 48, 40.5, and 30.5 cm).
- Form the strips into rings by taping the two ends of each strip together.
- Tape the rings to the cardboard strip, leaving at least 2 inches (5 cm) between each strip

## PROCEDURE

- Place your ruler on a flat, clean surface.
- Place your cardboard sheet (with rings attached) on the same surface, perpendicular to your ruler, so that the short end of the cardboard is nearly touching the ruler. Line up one edge with the 3-inch (7.5 cm) mark on the ruler.
- Gently move the cardboard about 2 inches (5 cm) along the length of the ruler, then move it back. Do this slowly a few more times. Notice the movement and shape of each paper ring as you move the cardboard. *Are all the rings moving? Do some rings move more than others? Which ones move the most? Which ones move the least? What happens to the shapes of the rings as you move the cardboard?*
- Repeat the movement, but this time move the cardboard slightly faster. Again, pay attention to what the paper rings do as you move the cardboard. *Do different rings move when you increase the speed? What happens to the shapes of the rings when you increase the speed of the cardboard? If more than one ring is moving, are they moving together (in synchrony)? Are any of the rings not moving? What happens to their shapes?*

- Repeat the movement, slowly increasing the speed that you move the cardboard. Make sure to keep the movement to 2 inches (5 cm). Every time you increase the speed of the movement, notice the effect on the rings. Notice whether the rings are moving and also whether their shapes change as you increase the speed. Keep increasing the speed to try to get all of the rings to move. *Which ring was the last to move? Which ring was the first to move? What changed about the movement of the big ring as you increased the speed? What changed about the movement of the small ring as you increased the speed? What changed about the shapes of the rings as you increased the speed of the movement? Were you ever able to get all the rings to move back and forth at the same time?*

- Try to find the resonant frequency for each ring. Increase and decrease the speed that you move the cardboard, watching to see the point where each ring seems the most excited, where that ring's movement is stronger and clearer than the other rings. Test to see if you can find a speed where only the smallest ring moves, then see if you can find the speed where only the biggest one moves. Test if you find a speed where all the rings move together. *Which ring seems to move the most at lower speeds? Which one moves the most at higher speeds?*

- Repeat the activity, but this time try moving the cardboard in 6-inch (15 cm) increments back and forth. Pay close attention to what happens to the rings as you slowly increase the speed of the movement. *Which ring moves first when you move the cardboard 6 inches (15 cm)? Is it the same ring that moved first when you moved the cardboard 2 inches (5 cm)? What happens to the shapes of the rings when you increase the distance of the movement? Is it easier or more difficult to get all the rings to move when you're moving the cardboard 6 inches (15 cm) back and forth?*

- Repeat the activity, moving the cardboard back and forth by 9 inches (23 cm), then 12 inches (30.5 cm). Pay attention to which rings move first and which rings move last at each distance. Also notice the shapes of the rings and how they change as you move the cardboard faster at each length. *How do the sizes of each ring relate to the distance of movements?*

## SCIENCE FAIR IDEA

Repeat this activity, but now hold the board above the table and move it up and down. Experiment with increasing the speed and distance that you are moving the cardboard. Notice how this affects the shape and movement of the rings.

## SCIENCE FAIR IDEA

Repeat this activity using different materials to make the rings. Some materials you might try include aluminum foil, thin floral wire (be sure to ask for an adult's help!), and paper with different thicknesses. Notice how the stiffness of the material affects the rings' movements and shapes.

## OBSERVATIONS AND RESULTS

Did you notice that at each distance, each ring seemed to have a favorite speed—a speed where that ring in particular seemed to have a stronger movement than the others? This is what we expect to see. The largest ring has the most mass, and it is also the floppiest (or least stiff). Just like with the low E guitar string, having more mass means the biggest ring has the lowest resonant frequency. Therefore, when you were moving the cardboard slowly, the biggest ring was probably more dynamic than the other rings. In contrast, the smallest ring has the smallest mass and is the least floppy (or the most stiff). As a result, the small ring has a higher resonant frequency and was the most dynamic when you were moving the cardboard faster.

If you tested different speeds of the movement, you might have noticed that at least some of the rings had more than one resonant frequency. For example, the big ring vibrated strongly when you were moving the cardboard slowly, but as you sped up it did not move as well. Then, when you got fast enough, the big ring seemed to get going again! This is because the rings (like many objects) have multiple resonant frequencies. If you pay close attention, however, you will notice that the shape of the big ring is different at the low resonant frequency compared with the higher one. At the low frequency, it flattens itself out, whereas at the high one, it might almost look like a square!

As you increased the distance of the movement, the resonant frequencies didn't change, but it was probably easier to see how the rings changed shape in response to the movement. If you moved the cardboard up and down, you probably noticed the rings followed this movement—instead of moving side to side, they seemed to get skinny and fat. The biggest ring still has the lowest resonant frequency, but you might have noticed that it was a little harder to get the smallest ring to move compared with when you moved the cardboard side to side. This is because when you're moving the board up and down, the cardboard is adding its own stiffness to the rings, making them less floppy in that direction.

## CLEANUP

**Put away your materials, and throw out any scraps.**

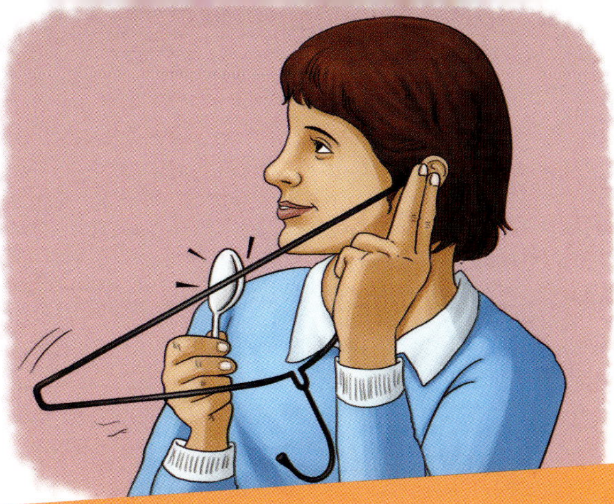

# Hanging Around with Sound
## Make Your Own Secret Bell!

DO YOU HEAR WHAT I HEAR? MAKE SOUND WAVES THAT ONLY YOU CAN HEAR WITH THIS SIMPLE, SECRET BELL!

Have you ever tried making "walkie-talkies" using a long piece of string and two tin cans? If you have, you know that they work surprisingly well—at longer distances, you can hear people better through the cans and string than you can through the air! In this activity, we're going to use the same concepts to build a personal bell—one that makes sounds that only you can hear!

### PROJECT TIME

45 to 60 minutes

### KEY CONCEPTS

Physics
Sound waves
Vibration
Hearing

## BACKGROUND

If you've ever been near a speaker with a loud bass (or heard a car drive by with the radio turned up), you may have experienced a "buzzing" feeling in your body caused by the loud noise. This isn't your imagination; the sounds we hear are actually vibrations traveling through the air—or through other materials, as we'll observe in this activity.

Most of the sounds we hear come to us through the air. When your friend calls your name, your friend's vocal chords cause vibrations in the air, which travel through it as a sound wave and arrive at your ears. Sound waves, however, can travel through other materials, too, and in fact many materials are much better than air at transmitting sound! You can experience this for yourself by gently tapping a metal fork or spoon against a countertop and listening to the sound. Next, put your ear to the countertop and tap the counter again with the fork or spoon. The sound should be much louder because the counter is better than air at transmitting the sound vibrations caused by the tapping!

The difference in how well a material can transmit sound is determined by the material's density, or how closely packed the molecules that make up the material are to one another. Imagine a row of dominoes. If the dominoes are far apart, one or two of them can fall over, but the rest will remain standing. If the dominoes are close together, one domino falling over will bump into the next one, which will bump into the next one, and the dominoes will fall down in a traveling wave. This is similar to how a sound wave travels; If the molecules are close to one another, they will bump into each other more often and the vibration will move through them more efficiently. Solid objects, such as metal desks and even string, have molecules that are packed together much more closely than the molecules in air.

## MATERIALS

- String
- One unpainted metal hanger
- Scissors
- Metal fork or spoon
- An adult helper

## PREPARATION

- With the help of an adult, cut two lengths of string, each about 2 feet (0.6 m) long.

- Tie one end of each string to a different corner of the base of the metal hanger. When you hold the hanger up by the strings, the hook part should be pointing toward the ground.

## PROCEDURE

- Hold the hanger by the hook in one hand, and use your other hand to tap the metal fork or spoon against the hanger. Notice the sound that it makes. *How long does the sound last? Would you describe it as "sharp" or "dull"? What other words would you use to describe the sound?*
- Gently place one corner of the hanger (where you tied one piece of string) to the small flap of skin just in front of your ear, closing off the ear canal. (You don't need to press hard!)
- Using the hand that isn't holding the hanger (or asking an adult to help you), gently tap the metal fork or spoon against the hanger again. Notice the sound this makes. *Is the sound different when the hanger is pressed against your ear compared with when you were holding it in the first step? How long does it last? What words would you use to describe this sound?*
- With the help of an adult, take one of the pieces of string tied to the hanger and wrap it around your index finger a few times. Wrap the other string around the index finger of your other hand.
- While you hold the hanger away from your body by the two strings, have your adult helper gently tap the hanger with a metal spoon or fork. Notice the sound this makes. *Is the sound different than in the earlier steps? How long does it last? How would you describe it?*

- Press your index fingers (with the hanger assembly attached) carefully on the small flaps of skin just in front of your ears, gently closing off the ear canals without putting your fingers into your ears. Allow the hanger assembly to swing freely from your fingers in front of your body, hook pointed toward the ground. Don't let the hanger or the string touch anything (except where the string is tied to your fingers).
- Have your adult helper gently tap the metal fork or spoon against the hanger. (Just tap once.) Notice the sound that this makes. *Is the sound different when the hanger is floating in the air compared with when you were holding it in your hands during the first two steps? How long does it last? What words would you use to describe the sound?*
- Gently swing the hanger so that it bangs lightly against something hard, such as the edge of a counter or table. Notice the sound that this makes. *Is the sound different when the hanger is pressed against your ear compared with when you were holding it in the first step? How long does it last? What words would you use to describe this sound? Do you notice anything about the strings after you bang the hanger against something? Are they moving? What type of movement?*
- Keeping your index fingers pressed on your ears, use your other fingers to grab the strings in your hands. Repeat the previous step, swinging the hanger into something hard. Notice the sound that this makes. *Is the sound different when you're holding the string in your hand compared with when it is hanging from your fingers?*

## SCIENCE FAIR IDEA

With your index fingers still pressed against your ears, try banging the hanger against something hard, then grab the strings right in the middle of the sound. *How does holding the strings change the sound you hear?*

## SCIENCE FAIR IDEA

Repeat the activity using another metal household item, such as a cooling rack, metal salad tongs, or a butter knife. *How does the sound change with the different items?*

## OBSERVATIONS AND RESULTS

When the hanger was hanging freely from your fingers, did you notice that the sound produced by tapping against it had more resonance (a deep, full, vibrating quality of sound)? It should have sounded more like a bell or gong when it was hanging from the string compared with when you held it or pressed it against your ears and tapped it.

Why did you hear different things? As we discussed in the background, sound vibrations can travel more easily through some materials than others. When the hanger assembly was hanging freely in front of your body, tapping the hanger caused it to vibrate. These vibrations traveled up the string and into your fingers, then through them into your head. When you held the hanger away from you and tapped it, the vibrations traveled through air to get to your ears. From this activity, you can tell that the string and your fingers are much better sound transmitters than the air around you!

When you were holding the hanger against your ear with your hand, the hanger couldn't vibrate as much (because you were holding it in your hand). Therefore, the sound was muted because fewer vibrations were produced. Holding the strings with your hands when you swung the hanger would have a similar effect. The strings couldn't vibrate as much, and therefore the sound waves were not transmitted as efficiently to your ears.

## CLEANUP

Untie the string from the hanger, and put the hanger and fork or spoon away.

# Can You Kazoo?

MAKE YOUR OWN KAZOO—AND LEARN SOME PHYSICS TOO!

In the summer, you might find yourself at a parade, party, or fair. While you're there, you will probably be surrounded by sounds of all kinds: fireworks, music, and maybe even the famous (or infamous) sound of kazoos! Whether you like them or not, these little noisemakers are a great way to learn about the physics of sound. In this activity, you'll be investigating how kazoos work by building your own!

## PROJECT TIME

30 to 45 minutes

## KEY CONCEPTS

Physics
Sound waves
Membranes
Acoustics
Harmonics

## BACKGROUND

A kazoo is a very simple musical instrument. It's made up of a hollow pipe with a hole in it. The hole is covered by a membrane that vibrates, resulting in a buzzing sound when people sing, speak, or hum into the pipe. People have been making and playing kazoos for years. The first kazoos were made from hollowed out bones, with spider egg sacs used for the vibrating membrane!

Although a kazoo looks and feels more like a flute or clarinet, it's actually most closely related to a drum. As the player sings, speaks, or hums into the open end, their vocal cords create sound waves that travel through the instrument. As they travel through the tube, some of the sound waves bounce off the walls of the instrument. This change in direction can add harmonics to the sound of the player's voice (depending on the material of the tube). However, most of the sound waves strike the membrane, causing it to vibrate. This vibration adds resonance or harmonics to the sound and creates the characteristic buzzing that we associate with the kazoo.

In this activity, you will experiment with sound using a kazoo you can make yourself from materials around your house.

## MATERIALS

- Empty cardboard tube, such as an empty paper towel or toilet paper tube
- Plastic grocery bag
- Aluminum foil (square sheet, approximately 4-by-4 inches [10-by-10 cm])
- Paper towel sheet (square sheet, approximately 4-by-4 inches [10-by-10 cm])
- Rubber band
- Sharpened pencil
- Scissors
- An adult to help

## PREPARATION

- Use the scissors to cut a 4-by-4-inch (10-by-10 cm) square from the plastic grocery bag.

## PROCEDURE

- Try saying a few words out loud. Draw out the sounds and listen to your voice. Say "KAAA-ZOOO!" Pay attention to how your voice sounds.
- Put one end of the cardboard tube to your mouth so that it is touching the skin around your mouth but not touching your lips.
- With the tube to your mouth, try speaking again. Draw out your words and make a lot of sounds. Say "KAAA-ZOOO!" Pay attention to the sound of your voice as it travels through the tube. *Does your voice sound different as it travels through the tube? What is different about it? Can you feel the tube vibrating as you speak?*
- Place the 4-by-4-inch (10-by-10 cm) square you cut from the grocery bag over one end of the tube. Use the rubber band to secure it firmly in place.
- Put the uncovered end of the tube to your mouth, and try speaking again. Make the same sounds you did before. Say "KAAA-ZOOO!" *Does your voice sound different with the plastic on the tube? What is different about it?*
- Have an adult help you use the sharpened pencil to poke a hole on one side of the cardboard tube, halfway between the two ends.
- Put the uncovered end of the tube to your mouth, and try speaking again. Make the same sounds you did before. Say "KAAA-ZOOO!" *Does your voice sound different than it did before you cut the hole? What is different about it?* Try covering and uncovering the hole with your finger as you continue to speak.
- While you're speaking through the tube, gently touch the plastic bag covering the end of the tube. *Can you feel the plastic moving? What happens if you try to press the plastic harder to prevent it from moving while you're talking? Does it change how your voice sounds?*

- Remove the plastic bag from the end of the tube, and replace it with the piece of aluminum foil. Use the rubber band to secure it in place.
- Put the uncovered end of the tube to your mouth, and try speaking again. Make the same sounds you did before. Say "KAAA-ZOOO!" *Does your voice sound different than it did with the plastic bag covering the end of the tube? If so, what is different about it?*
- Like you did with the plastic bag, while you're speaking through the tube, gently touch the aluminum foil covering the end of the tube. *Can you feel the foil moving? What happens if you try to press the foil harder to prevent it from moving while you're talking? Does it change how your voice sounds?*
- Repeat the activity using the paper towel to cover the end of the tube. Notice how the sound of your voice changes with the different covering.

## SCIENCE FAIR IDEA

Try different-size cardboard tubes. Notice how the sound of your voice changes with different-size tubes.

## SCIENCE FAIR IDEA

Try poking additional holes in the cardboard tube. *Does this change the sound of your voice when you speak into the tube?*

## OBSERVATIONS AND RESULTS

At each step of this activity, you changed the structure of the tube. You probably noticed that with each change, the sound of your voice changed as well.

In the first step, when you spoke through the tube, you may have noticed that your voice sounded deeper or more resonant. This is because when you speak, sing, or hum into the tube, some of the sound waves bounce off the walls of the tube, changing the direction from which and time at which they reach your ears. This adds harmonics to the sound, and the effect is dependent on the material of the tube. (Softer material will absorb the sound waves, making them quieter.)

After you placed the plastic bag over the end of the tube, you may have noticed that your voice sounded muffled compared with the tube with no plastic on the end. This is because the plastic created a barrier for the sound waves to pass through before reaching your ears, resulting in them losing energy along the way.

When you cut the hole in the tube, you may have noticed that it was easier to hear the sound of your voice. It also probably sounded amplified and more resonant. This is because the plastic at the end acts as a membrane, vibrating in response to your voice. The hole in the tube relieves the pressure inside the tube, allowing air (and sound) to escape and reach your ears.

When you repeated this activity with the aluminum foil and paper towel, you may have noticed that your voice didn't have the same vibrating quality as it did with the plastic bag. This is because neither the aluminum foil nor the paper towel is quite as effective as a membrane. The aluminum foil is less flexible than the plastic bag, so it did not vibrate as much as the bag did in response to your voice. As a result, sound may have bounced off the foil, but it did not amplify in the same way. In contrast, the paper towel was a less-effective membrane because it is too porous. Air—and thus sound waves—could pass directly through it without causing it to vibrate.

### CLEANUP

**Put away your materials, and throw out any scraps.**

# Making Sound Waves

TURN SOUND INTO SOMETHING YOU CAN SEE!

How well do you know your eardrums? You probably know that your eardrum is an essential part of your ear, allowing you to hear the world around you. However, why do we call it a drum? It turns out that calling it a drum is a very accurate description of what your eardrum looks like—and what it does inside your ear. To understand how your eardrum works, imagine using a drumstick to bang on a real drum and then touching the drum with your hand. When you do this, you can feel the vibrations moving through the drum material. Our eardrums work in a similar way, but instead of from the beat of a drumstick, our eardrums vibrate in response to sound waves hitting it. We can't see these sound waves with our eyes. However, we can see how they cause vibrations in things around us, just as they do in our eardrums!

## PROJECT TIME

30 to 45 minutes

## KEY CONCEPTS

Acoustics
Vibrations
Sound waves
Hearing

## BACKGROUND

What we experience as sound is actually a mechanical wave, produced by the back-and-forth vibration of particles in the air (or whatever medium is around our ears—remember that sound travels through water too!). To understand this, imagine (or try) clapping your hands underwater. As your hands move toward each other, they gather water, creating a space behind them that the surrounding water particles rush to fill. Once your hands meet, the water particles between your hands are squashed together. You can see the result of both of these events as ripples moving away from your clapped hands through the water. Sound waves travel through air in a similar way. When you clap your hands, you displace, or move, the air particles between and around your hands. This creates a compression wave that travels through the air (much like it did in the water). A continuous sound (such as the one produced by a tuning fork) is caused by the vibrations of the fork tines. The tines' vibrations repeatedly compress and displace the air particles around them, causing a repeating pattern of compressions that we hear as a single, continuous tone. The faster the tines move, the less time there is between each compression, causing a higher-frequency sound wave.

When this wave hits your ear, it encounters your eardrum. Your eardrum is a very thin membrane that acts as a barrier between the outside world and your inner ear. Although it protects the inside of your ear, your eardrum's real purpose is to transmit sound. When the sound waves hit your eardrum, they cause it to vibrate—the same way that a real drum vibrates when you hit it with a drumstick. The vibrations in your eardrum are then transferred via three tiny bones inside your ear into a fluid-filled chamber called the cochlea (pronounced KOK-lee-uh). Vibrations in your cochlea are transformed into electrical signals that your brain interprets as sound. We hear different sound pitches (highs and lows) based on the sound wave's frequency—the higher its frequency, the higher its pitch.

In this activity, you will be observing the vibrations caused by sound waves as they pass through a model membrane, just like the vibrations that go through our eardrums!

## MATERIALS

- Parchment or wax paper
- A large rubber band that will fit around the top of a glass bowl (An elastic headband works well, too.)
- A small glass bowl large enough to rest a Bluetooth speaker at the bottom

- Sugar or salt (To help you see the results better, you can use colored sugar sprinkles, or you can color the sugar or salt yourself with food dye.)
- A portable Bluetooth speaker
- A phone or other device that can connect to your speaker (For this activity, you will play one single tone at time from the device. There are several free tuner apps available as well as YouTube videos that you can use to play single tones from a phone. Be sure you have permission to add apps to the device.)
- Earplugs (optional)

## PREPARATION

- Place the speaker in the bowl; make sure it is on and connected to the phone or device you will be using.
- Cover the top of the bowl with a sheet of wax paper.
- Wrap the rubber band around the edges of the bowl to secure the paper in place.
- Sprinkle a layer of sugar or salt over the paper. Make sure that the granules are spread evenly across the paper; try to avoid piles.

## PROCEDURE

- Open the tuner app (or a YouTube video playing one single tone) on the phone or device. Start with the lowest frequency tone available. Set your volume to the lowest possible setting, and hit play.
- While the tone plays, observe the sugar or salt granules on the paper. *What do you notice about the granules? Are there any changes? If so, what are they?*

- Slowly increase your phone's volume. Each time you increase it, pause to observe the sugar or salt. *What do you notice? Have the granules changed? In what way?*
- Continue to increase the volume, observing any changes to the sugar on the paper. (Important: Keep your speaker volume within a comfortable range.) *What effect does increasing the volume have on the sugar or salt? What do you think is causing this change?*
- When you see an effect on the sugar or salt, try pausing the tone and then restarting it. *When the tone stops, what happens to the granules? What about when you restart the tone? Why do you think the tone has this effect on the granules? Do you notice any patterns in how the granules behave when the tone is playing?*
- Pause the tone, and reset the sugar or salt so that it is evenly spread across the paper again.
- Set your phone back to the lowest volume, and change the frequency of the tone that you are playing a higher frequency.
- Repeat the activity, slowly increasing the volume for this new tone. *How is the new tone different? Does it sound higher or lower? How does the new tone affect the granules? Is the effect different than what you observed with the first tone? If so, in what way? What do you think causes the difference between the two tones?*

## SCIENCE FAIR IDEA

Repeat the activity, trying different tones. Try to explore a wide range! Tip: Look up a video of "Chladni's experiment" and use the audio to try tones in your own activity!

## SCIENCE FAIR IDEA

Try the activity again, but this time replace the glass bowl with other household containers. *Does a cake pan work? What about a vase? What about a metal or wood bowl?* If you didn't see any results the first time, try using a deeper bowl, and try different sizes.

## OBSERVATIONS AND RESULTS

Did playing the tone cause the sugar or salt granules to move around on the wax paper?

As the sound wave travels through the wax paper, it causes the paper to vibrate. When you increase the volume of the tone, you are adding energy to the sound wave, resulting in larger vibrations. Eventually, these vibrations are large enough to move the sugar or salt on the paper.

You may have also noticed that the granules move in different patterns depending on the frequency of the tone. When the frequency of the tone changes, the vibration of the wax paper changes as well, resulting in the changing patterns of sugar or salt grains.

## CLEANUP

Wipe up any spilled granules, put away your materials, and throw out any scraps.

# THE SCIENTIFIC METHOD

The scientific method helps scientists—and students—gather facts to prove whether an idea is true. Using this method, scientists come up with ideas and then test those ideas by observing facts and drawing conclusions. You can use the scientific method to develop and test your own ideas!

**Question:** What do you want to learn? What problem needs to be solved? Be as specific as possible.

**Research:** Learn more about your topic, and refine your question.

**Hypothesis:** Form an educated guess about what you think will answer your question. This allows you to make a prediction you can test.

**Experiment:** Create a test to learn if your hypothesis is correct. Limit the number of variables, or elements of the experiment that could change.

**Analysis:** Record your observations about the progress and results of your experiment. Then, analyze your data to understand what it means.

**Conclusion:** Review all your data. Did the results of the experiment match the prediction? If so, your hypothesis was correct. If not, your hypothesis may need to be changed.

# GLOSSARY

**acoustics:** The qualities in a room that affect how well a person in it can hear things.

**biology:** A science that deals with living things and their relationships, distribution, and behavior.

**characteristic:** Relating to a special quality or appearance that makes an individual or a group different from others.

**circulation:** The movement of blood through the body.

**diameter:** A straight line that runs from one side of a figure and passes through the center.

**granule:** A small particle.

**harmonic:** A sound wave whose frequency is a whole-number multiple of the frequency of the same reference signal or wave.

**insulate:** To separate a conductor of electricity, heat, or sound from other conductors by means of something that does not allow the passage of electricity, heat, or sound.

**perception:** Understanding or awareness gained through the use of the senses.

**physics:** A science that deals with the facts about matter and motion.

**resonance:** When one object vibrating at the same natural frequency of a second object forces that second object into vibrational motion.

**sensor:** A device that responds to a physical stimulus.

**sequence:** The order in which things happen.

**short circuit:** An electrical connection made between points in an electric circuit between which current does not normally flow.

**sonorous:** Able to produce sound.

# ADDITIONAL RESOURCES

## Books


Albertson, Margaret E., and Paula Emick. *Music: The Sound of Science*. Vero Beach, FL: Rourke Educational Media, 2019.

Lacey, Jane. *Sound: Get Hands-On with Science*. London, UK: Franklin Watts, 2021.

Rake, Jody Sullivan. *What Is Sound?* London, UK: Raintree, 2020.


## Websites

**Discovery Education**
*sciencefaircentral*.com

**Exploratorium**
*https://www.exploratorium.edu/search/science%20fair%20projects*

**Science Buddies**
*https://www.sciencebuddies.org/science-fair-projects/project-ideas/list*

**Science Fun**
*https://www.sciencefun.org/?s=science+fair*

## Videos

**"Sound: The Science of Sound"**
*https://ny.pbslearningmedia.org/resource/ba1c1421-6d54-4044-98b7-496f325cccb7/sound/, PBS Learning Media, 4:02.*

**"What Is Sound?"**
*https://ny.pbslearningmedia.org/resource/what-is-sound-video/science-of-sound/, PBS Learning Media, 8:11.*

# INDEX


**A**
acoustics, 51, 56
adult helper, 7, 12, 34, 46–48
apps, 18–20, 58

**B**
biology, 11

**C**
cochlea, 57

**D**
decibel (dB), 17–20

**E**
eardrum, 12, 16, 56–57

**F**
frequency, 20, 23–24, 33–34, 39, 44, 57–60

**G**
granules, 58–60
guitar, 23–26, 28, 40, 43

**H**
hearing, 18, 20, 30, 45, 56
hertz (Hz), 20, 34

**I**
instruments, 23–26, 33–38, 40, 51–55

**K**
kazoo, 51–55

**M**
magnets, 5–9
material science, 27
membrane, 6, 51–52, 55, 57
metal, 28–29, 31, 46–49, 60
molecules, 6, 46
music, 5–6, 8–9, 51

**P**
particles, 12, 15, 34, 57
phone, 5–6, 17–20, 58–59
physics, 5, 11, 17, 23, 27, 33, 39, 45, 51
pitch, 6, 14, 20, 23–26, 28, 33, 37–38, 57
plastic, 12, 24, 28–29, 31, 34, 52–55

**R**
resonant frequency, 39–40, 42–44
rubber bands, 23–25, 34–38, 52–54, 57–58

**S**
scientific method, 4, 61
sound waves, 4, 6, 12, 14–15, 24, 33–34, 40, 45–46, 49, 51–52, 55–60
speaker, 5–9, 57–59

**T**
tone, 25, 28, 35, 37–38, 57–60

**V**
vibrations, 6, 12, 24–25, 27–28, 31, 34, 36–37, 39–40, 45–46, 49, 52, 56–57, 60
vocal chords, 34, 38, 46
voice, 17, 19–20, 24, 38, 52–55

**W**
water, 11–16, 24, 28, 57
wires, 6–9, 43
wood, 28–29, 31, 60

**Y**
YouTube, 58